Age of Glass

Age of Glass

Anna Maria Hong

Cleveland State University Poetry Center
Cleveland, Ohio

Copyright © 2018 by Anna Maria Hong

All rights reserved
Printed in the United States of America
Printed on acid-free paper

ISBN 978-0-9963167-9-8

First edition

22   21   20   19   18   5   4   3   2   1

This book is published by the Cleveland State University Poetry Center,
2121 Euclid Avenue, Cleveland, Ohio 44115-2214
www.csupoetrycenter.com and is distributed by
SPD / Small Press Distribution, Inc. www.spdbooks.org.

Cover image: *Leopold and Rudolf Blaschka's Glaucus longiccirus*, Guido Mocafico © 2013, courtesy
of Hamiltons Gallery.
Cover design: Amy Freels
Age of Glass was designed and typeset by Amy Freels in Mrs. Eaves with Avenir Next
Condensed display.

A catalog record for this title is available from the Library of Congress.

Recent Cleveland State University Poetry Center publications:

Poetry
The Hartford Book by Samuel Amadon
The Grief Performance by Emily Kendal Frey
My Fault by Leora Fridman
Stop Wanting by Lizzie Harris
Vow by Rebecca Hazelton
The Tulip-Flame by Chloe Honum
Render / An Apocalypse by Rebecca Gayle Howell
A Boot's a Boot by Lesle Lewis
In One Form to Find Another by Jane Lewty
50 Water Dreams by Siwar Masannat
daughterrarium by Shelia McMullin
The Bees Make Money in the Lion by Lo Kwa Mei-en
Residuum by Martin Rock
Festival by Broc Rossell
The Firestorm by Zach Savich
Mother Was a Tragic Girl by Sandra Simonds
I Live in a Hut by S.E. Smith
Bottle the Bottles the Bottles the Bottles by Lee Upton
Adventures in the Lost Interiors of America by William D. Waltz
Uncanny Valley by Jon Woodward
You Are Not Dead by Wendy Xu

Essays
A Bestiary by Lily Hoang
I Liked You Better Before I Knew You So Well by James Allen Hall

Translation
I Burned at the Feast: Selected Poems of Arseny Tarkovsky translated by Philip Metres and
    Dimitri Psurtsev

For a complete list of titles visit www.csupoetrycenter.com

CONTENTS

I

II

III

I

The glass is falling hour by hour, the glass will fall forever,
But if you break the bloody glass you won't hold up the weather.

—Louis MacNeice, "Bagpipe Music"

THE COPPER AGE

In the beginning, world stretched terribly
thin. World was wound about the wrist of an
ur-Cyprian who managed two valises.
The world was pure Copernican. The sun

felt weak. One case was made of teak and gas
boiled from the abysmal sea. The other
cached seven pairs of powdery, prolix
wings, which made the ring run ever longer

around the min's expansive, vanishing arm,
itself drawn and ductile as desire.
A heat consumed and consuming formed
this elemental gyre within gyre.

The world would crack extravagantly spent,
a shining exemplar or ornament.

A PARABLE

At the edge of the village roofed with mossy
slate, stood a hermitage, an embassy, and
a palace. Being spent, we chose to enter

the palace, a very busy place. Messy as we
were, we were treated like royals,
Class E, which entailed the following

advantages: being served muesli in vintage
glasses; being assuaged that the King's
boozy rhetoric would not become policy;

and three, having the opportunity to bless
the day's carnage in homage to the deceased
Queen. Such delicacies! For our wages,

we were pinned with corsages dense with
glossy leaves, which became permanent
appendages. A page waved to indicate

that it was time to go to the embassy,

where nothing memorable happened. Then

it was on to the hermitage, the last stage,

where we would presage the image of ecstasy

and thus emboss our legacies. We pledged

to finesse the fallacy of hedge and spillage

and erase the badge of unease around certain

engagements. We gauged our audience and the time.

We lost our accents and flimsy excuses in a gorgeous

cortège. We learned to parse our emphases.

We became quite adept. In the distance, always

the glass sea breaking. It was our time to savage.

THE PLATINUM AGE

Depression was all the rage. We were at
the end of a line and did not know it.
We rang and sent our hearts out. The fat fat
of the land was separating. The fit

got very fit. Obese morbidity
was slung in fluent plural-capitalist
suicide songs. Our currency pretty
much ripped. Our leaders, also maximalist

devourers, indiscriminate, though well
informed. We were still excellent readers.
We learned to help ourselves. An abridged spell
of fortune was about to be reordered,

shuffled like cards in a pre-war era,
as we wrote our memoirs in diamond on mirror.

THE IRON AGE

... blood forgery, a staple activity

in the winter months along with peeling

old roots scraped from autumn's cavity.

Not much cheer in this tower where the ceiling

is smeared with smoke and the pock of thinking.

Our keenest minds bone-homed in elegant

atrophy, always a bit hungry, sinking

our teeth figuratively in government

grants, a grass-fed side of bison to spur

creativity: a heat-seeking sword,

a cure for feelings of estrangement or

complicity, a way to blunt the need

for evidence of our humanity

and return the universe to light and speed.

THE BRONZE AGE

A giant man and woman strode the land
anticipating the arrival of
the gods but not believing in the end.
They were enormous beings hewn out of

frost and fire. By day, they strode across
the elemental greens and grays that formed
the captious clouds of their existence.
By night, they dreamt crepuscular dreams formed

at the hour mixing twilight. They were
incapable of recollection.
Each day to night was mute perfection,

and neither could they ken the future.
Horizoning and blaring sure erasure,
the gods were felt as distant pressure.

NEPTUNE FROST

I have tasted smoke angels on the tip
of oblivion. The angels turned me
like a face and gave me a new name, turned
my face like revolution. The moon swung free,

a headstone without a name. I was the cold,
cold King of the sea, star in my palm burning
like an anthem, like ice on the blue black
sea. I was the tourniquet moon churning

against the burning sea, cold as a soldier's
sleeping feet. Eye to eye, oblivion
turned her burning face, while I wrestled
my nature in the clearing, and a nation

burned like ice on revolving tongues,
turning like a stone where the red moon hung.

PLAINEST HYMN

The anti-Christ was good, but the Misogynist
was superhuman. An A-list antagonist,
not your quotidian vermin, the kind of beast
who makes women apologize to exist.

A nasty condition really feeling the grist
in one's soul grating like zest
on an open cut, or a gritty violin.
The song comes out thin and testy

in spite of all the protein one ingests.
Like a moron one persists, like a priest
or a catechist chanting at a bris.
The sermon becomes ingrown. To be

honest, it's a pain. The cruelest twist:
Protean strength won't move the Rubicon.

THE IVORY BOX

I am a cone on quartered tendrils, deaf
as an epitaph. Art is dead, but sponge
will take forever. I'm the holy stuff,
the nod blown up inside your head, an orange

meringue with lemon crust. I am the poppy
seed's frozen core, soft and hard as the son
of a silicon bust. An ice-shaved pear, top
knot, absorbing Jupiter's wife and moon.

Juno never looked better, draped in
lightly clarified weather, solid at
room temperature, a toga wrapped within
a hot, atomic enigma. My high, flat

raison d'être projects a hive of mouths:
replicant births to the north and south.

EUROPA

Seduced by the obvious. Borne forth
on a bunch of white bull too crass and flaw-
less to resist. A back like plunged surf.
A sun of terminal pump and paw.

All fatuous thought gone to one. The globe
reduced to glide and spun. The eye a ship
of sapped expanse. Eternity disrobed.
The bending of his blended bones. A grip

within my planted lunge. The inner pin
of infinite numb. Never thinking of home.
Obliterate elixir. Heat so thin.
And nothing outside the animalistic form.

The repeated rub of endless project.
The balance between us hung like logic.

10

Omikron to her Omega, Io
am I. From hollow to hello, grotto
to mondo, he followed. Then quicko, all moo
was I. She knew. For him, I was blotto.

Now doomed to loop his gassy bongo
like some dumb bean, pinto or garbanzo,
like one number in one bunkum bingo,
I fly the shoo in his falsetto

pie. Boo hoo hoo. I too can go commando,
Captain Neo, serve up coolio,
assume the form of a loon. Lo! Not so lame-o
like poor Cleo, all coo and brio

on the patio. I hoof my halo
like one swift bolo. I owe you.

CIRCE

The fuck you in me crosses the street to
avert the fuck you in you. This fuck you
subverted gnaws the hasp of my liking you
until I don't really like you and woe

is we. The former us in me would like
to be jettisoned too or at least have
a deck to leap from. The you I knew sticks
around in spite of the editions luck

would make of me and you. My memory
is quite specific: fucking you in the
garden at night, at last. Fucking you-me

Edenic with no future like the present.
A good fuck you to give fucking some love
too, looking back when it hasn't happened yet.

PANDORA

To be adorable and thus worshipped
to the world's eight corners, all-gifted and given
to hot Prometheus' less foxy brother who said,
"I don't mind getting hurt," blurting it out

and smiling like he'd earned a piece of candy.
It took me ages to get over hating
the gods who made me. In the meantime, more
mundanity: humanity prospering,

blah, blah, blah. Meanwhile, they kept shoving
that thing in front of me, moving it around
the bedroom so I'd see it upon waking:

six surfaces, all containment all the time.
"Sure as metaphor's a whore," said E.
I flipped my lid and changed my name to Sally.

PERSEPHONE

I want to be stiff as a board, light as
a feather, driven like the snow. Hell is
a den of done cliché, but hey, no one
is hotter than Hades. Manor and man

are thick as a brick if you get my drift.
They say that every curse contains a gift,
and sometimes they hit the nail on the head.
Believe it or not, I've been better off dead.

Life was a journey unpredictable as weather.
I sprang from someone who hurt like a mother.
The seed was smooth as silk and sweet as honey.
It made me feel filthy and rich as money.

The seed was my ticket to plummet. Each
to each, the fat lady sang for me.

CHORUS

Am I coming from damage? Has loss been

my privilege to know? Does pain restate

untenable burden? Is the neck the stem

of the soul? Is stability a gate?

Shall I repeat the species' evolution

in my developing person? Do I

develop like film in a small brown

lake? Am I seer and gravel or do I

taste like half an animal from a former

Iron Age? Am I to mutate misery

from ruin? Will metal commute malignant fire?

How many are present today? Are they

patient or witness? Tell me, dear Maker, and

does anyone here have the means to amend?

MEDEA V / DEPARTURE

Whale-road. The path to Athens glittered
with blues, and as we rolled, I dove under
with those broad, gray backs through each wave. What mattered
now? A clutch of minnow breaking surface asunder,

the sun on my face burning like potential,
salt in my hair, my skin. The knowledge of you
unable to locate the source of denial.
The world billowing below this normal vessel.

The spray and scent and speed. A strafe of white
gulls peeling over the hull's wall, blooming like
bare streaks. A hint of fire on the horizon ...

Upon leaving the Kingdom where every hero's
a victim and vice versa: the V-shaped flight
of something rising in rows and rows and rows.

II

And my husband stood stock-still, as if she had been Medusa, the sword still raised over his head as in those clockwork tableau of Bluebeard that you see in glass cases at fairs.

—Angela Carter, "The Bloody Chamber"

I, SING

out of this world & out of time & out

of love & out of mind & out of the

pan & out of butter, out of anger

& out of mother, out of the cradle

& out of pocket, out of space & out

of cash & out of change & out of sight

& out of range & force of habit

& out of oil & out of whack & out

of water & Damascus, out of courtesy

& out of shock & out of duty

& out of turn & out of tune & out of line

& out of the ground & out of his gourd

& out of all the possible solutions,

out of the ashes & conviction

AGE OF INCREMENT

After Percy Bysshe Shelley

Liberticide optimized in an age
of glint democracy—a pretty line
for a pretty time continuously engaged—
the King's flag flown above the sign

of the dove—our hawkish Queens keening
the horn on a third front—one occupation
blunts another and another—meaning
gummed in purple doublings, set to stun

dialogue to silence—to recession
from attention to what matters, dies—will,
individual, broken by the extension
of hope and its perhaps inevitable

dilution—interest dipped, tinted, rinsed, and fenced,
looped and linked like a tarnished chain reaction.

SPUN

The very people are not very nice.
The very people feel disdain, disgust
even, for the persons who by choice
and skill manage to pull hand over fist

from the ditch of chance. Recall the tiny
red man who saved the Miller's daughter, spinning
thatch to gold. Gold! The engine of alchemy
was rage. The small man's history of winning

was long but irrelevant. Remember what
he wanted? Someone's child. (Normalcy.)
He delivered the strange: exactly that
which was required for her security.

He notched quotidian stuff to something
tough, wrought, and so much desired by the King.

CIN CITY

In the dumb Kingdom of fear and trembling,

the person with the see-through slipper knew

enough to split before the other one

dropped. Step and carry, bitter and better,

the girl with the slipper knew better than

to carry on as if all shoes were fit

to be tried. Split-splat, the girl was violet

in a realm of mimic green. *Tremble and spot,*

better to have tied myself in knots,

thought the girl with the one good shoe. Slip her

a bitter, the person with the see-through

boot renamed the Kingdom "fear" after her

most beloved shade of green. The good spot

split, as if immaculate, and slipped into an amble thing.

NURSERY SIGN

There was an Old Woman who lived in a
shoe. Had so many children and a husband
to boot. A gnarléd patience was her friend.
The toe was cramped with acumen and a

silver-plated flute that no one knew how
to play. Each bairn she birthed was given chance
to push the buttons harking such romance
that would unlace the shoe that kept allow-

ing them to stay. Freedom was a short step
away. Each babe assayed the silver tube,
which slept inert and solid as a club

until the noted day the woman snapped
her gums and said, "No music will uncap
the shoe. We must unhorn it with ourselves."

F, H & G

I'm a virgin in a dirty apron

holding a pair and a black stripe. Will you

tell me about your troubles re: the letter

F? First let's find a future infant matron

and a falling apart version of the f***** up

fairy fiction of the fraternal Grimm.

At forest's fringe, our agon begins,

as fur-clad, feral children fling crumbs from

fastidious limbs. Full of fail, unfettered,

these orphans are furious, as only those who

find themselves flung can be. Their futile litter

has fueled their hunger for the candy house of

revenge. These newfound foundlings, forsaken twins—

one fat, one finally fed up—give fate a firm shove.

A FABLE

Purveyor of rot and whatnot,
entrepreneur of I forgot,
with wrists hard as hammers—
that birthmark a slot—

grip it, strip it, flip it hard—
ramp my shard.
If fear be sexy, a synch
& a match—

Gone the way of wax & worms—
gone like November 2011—
sweet by nature, mean by culture—

"Goodbye, luck, you idiot,"
said the Fox to the Grapes.
"I love you," replied the Grapes.

I, NOUMENAL

For the character and the content. For
the combination of the two. By which
formula may I speed your healing? I
remove the rods of genius glowing to go

a-historical. I am prodding the sand
like a bad, bad man. Like a raper with
a switch and a banner, one in each hand.
I court my violence. I play ball on that court.

The King is bored by my antics, which are
after all, useless. "Bring in the Minister
of Function," he declares in front of me.
I become the Minister of Implication,

my senses enriched as uranium
and no less stable.

I, TONIC

Give me liberty through diction and
fiction refined as sugar and oil—
product and process, again, again.
Who gains? What gives? The sum of my

positions, poisons, margins, intentions
to be home free—the truth as I take it—
hard as beauty, soft as goodness—
acid bath elixir—

my native environs—stripped as
wire, bare as thread and dead
as an engine—embraced, reduced—
the grain now the sum of me—

the kernel, my captain, ship, and crew.
I am so small. Article—amber—sand—

THE THREE SPINNING-WOMEN

I dreamt of the tropics and no one offering

to pay for gas. Done with iambics, I wrote

the following instead:

> In the cellar of a tower of a very cold

palace, three crones are spinning Fate and thread

for a future Princess too inept

to meet the Queen's behest. Or is it craft?

The spinsters run wonders for the delightedly duped

Queen, who has her son wed the gifted woman.

The crones—quite hideous—want nothing other

than to be at the wedding as familiar,

accepted guests. The bride obliges. The groom

asks how they got to be so ugly. "It was toil,"

explains one. "Cord and wheel stretched thumb, lip, and heel."

I didn't write this tale. It's by the Brothers Grimm.

I, SORORICIDE

After William Shakespeare

We so royal, we do hate thee unanimously.

All things being equal, you disgust us.

How do we hate thee?

Let us count:

(1) Cut.

(2) Cut your penis.

(3) You talk too much.

Queen for an hour but worth it!

Blind like your loyalty

yet still so naïve.

We would like to enjoy your weakness.

No eyes but your P will keep you.

And your good son. We'll kill ourselves over

the bad one.

THE RED BOX

I have a little husband. Keep him in
a box. He sleep with rust about his meat,
his tender crust a clutch. His ten-fold skin
so *roi*. He want and vaunts I beat and beat.

I half a little husband. Keeps him in
a box. He sleeps with rust *avant* his meat,
his shiny crust a clutch. His two-putt skin
so viney. Vic and then he vow. I beat

him to a finish. Finish blood and blue.
I tell him: Now flip over. He cannot
unpaste his shoe. *To haste, to haste, to too.*
To make my bandy slide inside the slot,

I keep him well and oil. I make him stuff
the blade all down > he calls himself a knife.

CLUE

Miss Scarlet in the foyer with the hot

pink slit. Oh, vaguely Asiatic. O

nimble little quick. Peacock knots

a feather twisted at the wrist. Her co-

habitual partner fluffs and battens

his bitch. Mustard's in the pantry, stocking

up on ice. He downs a neat Manhattan,

and rubs his impeccable monocle

once or twice. White and Green split an orange

beneath the disco's blurred ball. Off- and

bottle-, off they toddle, filling a syringe

with dirt. Professor Plum strokes the coffin

he thinks will hold his head. Cradles the phone

like an infant in the basement of the dead.

REVEILLE

From captor to native and cradle to eve,

           waking and waving ourselves, our sleeves

in the cosmic breeze that ships us

           to shape. O! harness, O! dumb dorsal purpose—

bluesmocking Alice alone in her palace, which happens

           to be a hole—to be is to drop & grab

the bottle off the shelf to have something

           to peruse along the fall. O! All the world's a stage

in dishevelment. We bust each increment

           to the best of our implement, to be fit is to be

part of the service of render of temper

           of hull of fin

O! Lark

      O! Manna   O! Roll

AURA

I was erased as a morning face

and slim as a pocket. I was steady

as dust and feathers blown hard across

a mackerel lake. I was bloody

chuffed in three-quarters, but I wasn't empty

anymore. I was tone, pause, energy.

I was a good stiff pour. Come and tempt me,

mimetic. Come shine on all fours. Urge me

untoward. A Maker made to tell. The day

began as terminal and ended so

tight. How I wanted to be the only.

I did not want another to

replace my mine. No, I did not enjoy

"the process" of effacement, though it was a start.

THE HOOD

I am one crack dirigible, full of
hot He. I've got Doppler vision zippered
to my engine, pulsing the limits of
expansion. Over the hill and through the paper

to Grandmother's house I go. "Granny,"
says me, "what big." "Don't be so hyper,"
says s/he, "the better to kill you figuratively."
"Not now," says me. "I'm busy. What this caper

slash tragedy needs is a new beginning, middle,
and ending. I cut you and your disguises
out of the running. Little Dread Hiding Could! This riddle
resolves its discontent by shifting pieces

from hip to hop horizon. This blimp has blown
past smithereens to map a ready wave.

THE WHITE BOX

Circle, circle, circle, and the bang is

buck geometry. The figure fronts full

fanatic symmetry. Disarray

arranges the gun of the lock. An eye

under ocean is still an eye. The wall

is studious narcotic. Slant reuses

the cant of the box. A palindrome pulse

recalibrates luck. The surface breaks

attention away from the point of born again.

Color on prayer. The core purls hardly parsed.

Motion scopes permission. Harmony

is a thrust. From arrow to vapor and pin

to bust, the helidrome ritualizes

felt logic, scraping escape from the blast.

SALOMÉ

It's a cinch and a rack, this Asiatic
attack of cryptic fever, which leaves me
winching my hunches and bunching my haunches
in an avalanche of drench. Unblock

your rustic reticence, my curly head
Comanche. Unpack your filthy white worship
in this quick trench. Shellac my bench.
Line my sack. I give you *carte blanche*

to stick that branch. Evac the ranch, crack
my conch, my embalmed, yellow-eyed ascetic.
Stop flinching. Look at me, not as a heretic

but as a wrench to twist your hermetic
inch from its attic of static piety,
your monastic track. Synch to me.

MOON TO SUN

Corona's at the edge of what's acceptable.
My Artemesian well will cover your stare
though I could swear, you won't feel it. Table
and chair. Development, return. We are

the ultimate binary pair, but only
from one perspective. I am a much smaller
massive object, cool, internal, free
of my own light. My gravity will collar

your value. You will darken me to pure
black splendor, as I bury your power
behind me. I am not quite as discrete

as I ought to be. You have everything
I want, and you will give me more than what
I want to need when I make you my ring.

KING WORM

I do, I do, I do. I do love you.

Do I do. I do love you. I love, I

do you love. I love, do you. I, I,

I do you love. Love do I you. You do

love I. I, I, you, you, I you do love.

Do you, I do. Do you do. You do you.

You, you. I, you. You, you, you. You. Do you.

I do. I do. I do. I do. I love

you, love. I love love. Love, I do. I love,

love I. I do. I do. I you do I.

I. I do. I, I, I. I, I. Do I.

Love. You, I. I, you. I. You. You love love,

you do. Love, do you. You do. Love do love.

Do I love you. I you, you. I you you.

QUEEN EGG

Love the man that loves the heart that loves the
ring that binds me. Love the ruse that loves the
hook that tries so hard to find me. Love, love,
love. Love the tune that rues the June she fell

from the bower. Rapunzel, let down your tower.
Love the rhyme that marks the time she saves
your assignation. Love the man that furs
the line. Love the tense that cures the brine. Love

the guise that gives rise. Love the flesh of the
sign. Love the man who loves the mind of more
tomorrow. Love regret's long furrow. Love
the liege as would my lord would have.

Love the give of summer, ever.
Love the soar of the notion.

EVER YOUR MATE

Better believer makes her circuit o'er
the planet, maneuvering through pure
hate, shielded by her fur hat and etiquette's
quiver, her chariot a former doormat

that glides above glint and river, powered
by increment; tiny, ancient cadavers and a surfeit
of fever inflating like an oeuvre. Circling
the Tower in indirect light, she pulls

the lever to cast her ballot for the Tarot's
head-first diver, enigmatic bait,
a sure bet in her net opinion. Rover
at the clavier, riven averrer and tourniquet

remover, glutting on slivers from the striver's
market, surfing the quaver like a bouquet flower.

THE HOLOGYNIC

I sought new strangers under cover, a cloak
of normalcy cinched at my throat. I let
the cape slip through the neck of time. It looked
like a sail collapsing. I felt my teeth

tightening, my right ear ringing a volley
of hunting songs. I tried to hide again
but the veil was gone, so down I sallied
through dip and valley green with invitation.

My skin grew mossy, cool as river water
and soft as blood. My eyes enameled over:
dark, bright, and keen. I could go anywhere.
I had no fear. The gods I'd known were dead

inside me, where such things apparently
matter. I was ferociously happy.

THE NIGHTS

—listen, I have listened to a thousand
and some terrible stories, each one
a marble spun from parable, sand, and
blast. The morals vary, but not really:

Genies are mean outside the bottle, so
wish within their limits. The person who
observes the thief will reap the stolen gold.
When the King (clever, trapped) summons you,

pretend to be a log. Leap into the fire
for faster transportation. Be nice to animals.
Trick the ifrit into getting small
enough to fit inside his portable

home, then fling it to the ocean's bottom
among the coral whose stories have no lessons.

Through this glass:
a new world.

—Korean proverb

THE EMPRESS

I built an enormous happiness from
babyhearts and sand. Then feeling whorish,
I left the palace of the Heavenly Emperor,
out the cloud gate, sword in hand. Some

would say I fled. I think of it as rolling over
a great abyss. Asparagi root, clover,
Japonici *(mai men dong)*, and some other
ingredients I can't remember mothered

me along. It's true. I realized it too
upon erecting and fleeing. There never
was a man. I had swallowed his temper

like the formula he was. Then feeling blue,
I left the palace of the Heavenly Emperor,
out the cloud gate, clutching a mirror and a will.

SNOWEM

The world has burned her skin to make another.

Branches like the hair of the mind become

an ocean in a pond, a bottle on

a river, a drop of hum. The idiom

of visual perception scratches gray

on gray, which I relive as beautiful,

stark, persistent. There is snow

on the ground lying like an annulled

agreement, *yes* transmuted to small ice.

Let's imagine we never began. Can

I have my *un-* back? The snow lies there

like a pull, still simile for ocean

or brain or blaze or skin. The snow is sick

of us, a powdered pill, tapped analgesic.

VA-VA PSALM

The gorgeous schwa of bonny *printemps* is
no *terra firma* for bourgeois true champs
salaamed up in solemn *joie de vivre.* Pass
the velum. This phylum's slummed to the edge

of aurora. Hark the new era, its blue lamp
a column of spark and ruin like Maw
and Paw, those two villains in the raw, verb/nouns
crossing their functions. Tote the totem. Hook

'em torn like a toe clamp on *primavera,* a swamp
of freedom akin to flora effulging like *exempla*
under the aqua patina of a northern
borealis. What a forum. What a mass. Bloom

a planetarium or a sherpa *qua* valium ferrying the blahs,
a chrome dome harem through the chutzpah of time.

MUSE & ME

The dreaded holidays are upon us.
We're done as turkeys with their heads popped
off. We're alert like legs tied up in truss.
You're the stuffing. I'm the maple syrup

someone forgot. You're the hand-dipped
roulade. I'm the undigested remark.
Fuck this! We're too much alike. I'm a cup
of gravy ladled over light and dark.

Sit down and eat. Please do assume the worst
of me. If I were you, I wouldn't take it
personally. I'd like a sliver of remorse
to go with my undercooked regret.

I'm full. The dog ate my napkin. One less
thing to toss in composting. Work, work.

CHAMPION UNDER WOOD

"*Ma beauté*, some men are continents, others,

trinkets." So said some French philosopher

or would have said, if he weren't so sexist,

but let's turn to our friend the novelist,

who'd already forgotten every aspect

of *Fear and Trembling* except for that bit

about the Merman—how Danish, how

totally Hans Christian. Half-fish. You

know the type, and in the particular

scene she was drafting someone would vanish.

She knew that much about drift and finish.

Tapping like a casket, she alone was the boss of her,

and that book would be her most cherished to date.

"Some summer," she wrote. She was thirty-eight.

WINTER ENTRY

After Ted Berrigan's "Sonnet XVIII"

Dear Phil, hello. It is 3:18
p.m. Outside my room, Atlantic sounds
of gray, headless dreams of gradual green
thrum in December gloom. In my skull, drowned

luster, cool disaster enlivening
the primal bed. Of Niki de Saint Phalle
responding. "Deliquescence," she said. Sing
it! And made an Xmas tune. You know, Phil,

this afternoon and every one dives in,
synched to that diurnal dryness. Them
again, again. And now without season,
I almost dread nothing, paranoid/calm

my new milieu. Your message: delivered.
I like to beat men up! At night, I heard.

CASSANDRA

I was about as wanted as a pang,

the kind in which

you know you're not wound but fang,

not nun but perve, not helping hand but ditch . . .

Thus my popularity and hyper-

marketability in the personal

arena, though that's not my problem either.

My problem is I'm shy. My arsenal

all organic matter: entrails, birds, skulls.

Or pattern, gleam, and some weird feeling that

I get to follow duly like a devil

fish and her probe. The subject of this portrait

is neither loathsome nor appealing but

is rather pleased because I say it.

PSYCHE

The smell of the man was ash and mechanical.

We wore our filth like a summer jacket.

The chair was not at all comfortable.

The table was missing an important nail,

or maybe the floor was bent. I couldn't

locate my rhythm, as if I'd forgotten that

it was the first. Art happened in tiny increment

like painting a pinky toe pink again.

In the car I wanted you so bad, but on

the couch I was more interested in

my lack of focus and formal negligence, but

when you said, "I am ridiculush," that

consonant made me like you anew, but

just for a second. I was full of myself and remnant complication.

ECHO

says that heart is fine. Echo
channel is alright. Murmur equals
dip within the tin of fever few too
many or few too few. Internal

        error but innocent. Heart is
like a house, she says, with little rooms,
electric vents, and clapping, tiny fists
applauding loose division through. Distress

is liquid trails. A path is wound through some
and full. Joy and other passing guests
caress percussive coils of each vena
cava brut. *Confess, confess, confess.*

Each sluice leaves less and less to the whole
muscular, hollow mass, shaped like this.

THE PEACH BOX

Flesh of my flesh, off-color, nexus of pearl
and rot, an infant's muzzle, nourishment
and sunder, to be et, ah! Fresh emetic,
copric dissolve, entropic pop, stop shipment—

the fruit, the cut, asymmetrical hut,
my tropic of horn, your tropic of rinser,
the juice, the nut, concentric obligate—
hut, hut! Don't pick. And aromatic this,

empathic that, the flavor: ick hermetic—
Eurocentric, neurotic, but a hut is
a hut. Erotic, misanthropic jut,
longitude and lat for six years flat, eyes

wide slat, revise and stet, redress gigantic
pit, Atlantic roll and tuck, controlled tick.

THE BLACK BOX

The work is a complex. The bachelor

must chop his own café. New fog recurs.

The palm enacts an island. Silence blurs

the violinist, as silver hair

susurrates the image. The conductor's

blades cut two rhythms. Heart

is a wet shirt. Two planted shoes refrain.

There is a beach for the slow gray cart.

A white horse weights the fisherman, as

frame stretches sand. The mother's youth is eyes

then flame.

The word erases.

The land is wave without a sound. A rise

lets breath bait breath. The work arrives, reverses.

THE GREEN BOX

The garden of earthly, sensual delight
excludes all impetus for usual caution.
Sumptuous fear, that primal temptation,
dissolves to pattern, paper-thin as light

through diamond-back. In the temple of suspension,
which is the mind, a supple tension expands
the skin stretched tight on spine and diamond,
contracting and repulsing light. The garden

of apple rot and sweet arable ruin
contracts again, an atavistic organ,
again, repulsing again, as the mind winds

its path through thick mortality, a line
in dust diverging purple origin,
a pause poised to envelop and remain.

BOX

Box is a river. Box is a nation.

Box is Noah's boat. Box is a bully

pulpit. Box is the antagonist in

a one-person show. Box is fully

present. Box is heart, blood, womb, and skin.

Box is metal, wood. Box is a dirty

glass. Box is plastic acting like estrogen.

Box is someone's murky

marginal notes. Is preverbal.

Is sand and curveball light.

Box is verbatim. Box is wall to wall.

Box is getting soggy. Box is for shit.

Box is a narc! Is your worst boss, your last

great lay, alas. Box is a half-day fast.

I, LYRIC

mid-March, perchance to sleep, to seem human

                   once   this is the end of the lattice as I

knew it   thought lined up

         like dolls, soldiers, black and red

         lack of sleep, a bump on the callous

of time   profoundly idiotic, strangely

                 gripping as if that manic jabber were

good-looking   flat morning on window

façade   the split world catching radial pool

            on fire but not here, not yet, and I am

dying as you are dying distracted, in debt

            to gods of will, malice, indifference,

sheer fathom, sheer plumb as depth,

    there is no bottom to feel, conceive

ZONE PLANNING

Arrived and a riven, *sans* belongings or

partisan leanings, our cloven-foot

universal citizen, former denizen

of blue heaven, finds itself groaning from

exhaustion, far flung, and pining for home's

clay oven, moaning chain gangs, flash frozen

smiles, hand-woven whips, and oolong tea.

But there was work to be done. It was time

to get even with that self-cloning clown,

that serene, haranguing, qigong lovin'

downer. "I'm powning that Pan-handling,

overdriven, father-son morning person.

This way station's mine for the canning. I'll give

them content for their meaning, damn-God-it."

MINOS

Time to lower you into the correct
division. Ring on ring, not my design,
but it is interesting. This will take
forever. Count backwards from ten. You might

feel a thing. It won't stop hurting.
I have to find it to assess it. Not
great, but it's what you had to work with. Like
a bean on a scale. A dried bean.

I'm writing this up for no one you know.
Yes, it's always chaos on the seventh
floor. There are worse situations, as I
think you knew. Beyond boring or reason

or weeping treason *ad infinitum*.
Did you love the burning world? I did.

YONDER, A RENTAL

Time to howl at the celestial sphere,

that full frontal silver dollar, the very

paintball of pallor and elemental other.

It's all or nada as noonnight's empanada

discloses her pretty quarter, the priest's collar

hung high on the hook of evening's fluent

wall. Hung like a juror bent on acquittal

who can't stall any longer, you're a cobbler

hawking copper coins in an Oriental

bazaar. The Sultan's power went horizontal

long, long ago. It's fine to be sentimental,

though there's no need to bother. Grab a handful

of shine like a disc of doll hair, a dollop

of Neufchâtel,

       valor and force, vital—

FOR SURE

For the natter and the symphony.
For the clatter and the verse. For the wefting
of the curse. For the stacked
tectonics. For the band mnemonic.

For the anachronicity. For the veiled
nudity. For the trad industry.
For the physical tap. For being sunk.
For good measure. For the stark raving

lack. For the atavistic act.
For the pouring glass. For the pitch.
For the drying nation. For cell, cull, and call.
For the trap agitation. For the force of daily mind.

For the peace of daily grind. For the carried
margin. For the feminine conclusion.

10 TO 2

Raise the hour and the glass—there is

beauty in the braggadocio. I break

my heart for you. My fast is no lament.

I break my luck in two: one for you

and two for me. My rumored blood,

my dynasty. The neck keeps pace. The horse

and I retouch the sky on clipped, brown wings.

To tell, rehearse, recede.

I raise a glass to the hour

you took the box from me. I raise my voice

inside your throat; I hum a viral children's

storyline, which has no native melody.

The arrow whistles through the weft. The watch

sets on a silver beam minutely attached.

DEMOGRAPH

Friends, Romans, Countrymen, Countryladies,
jinxed Jainists, born again Bahai, debunkers
of merit, people who do advanced Pilates,
exquisite corpses with two quarters, thunder

lovers, physicists with slipped discs, market
enthusiasts, professional complainers,
light nappers, philosophers of carrot/stick,
those who say, "I'm wearing new trainers,"

connoisseurs of pattern recognition,
dripping worshippers of the fog cult,
promise avoiders and renegers, men
who love a bony ass, the lame, the halt,

celibates with secret stocks of cash,
one-time receivers of the subtle flash.

LATIN MASS

The Buddhists have a saying: One soul's engine
is another's combustion. The Buddhists are nice
guys. Some Zen ones don't even drive. When men
of the cloth take a spin, figures of speech splice.

Giaour is "infidel" but not in Christian.
In Christian, it means "time well spent" or "fire
consumed." In Jewish, it connotes "to be the piston."
In Hindu, it becomes "tight like a tire."

In Heathen, we have a phrase for spirit
that has no equivalent in this milieu.
Actually, we have two. The first is: "Hear it
clicking, pull over before it kills you."

The second is something like: "The wheel
that rides a lot of small connected wheels."

AGE OF EVIDENCE

Twenty-first-century explorers challenge

the ocean of inevitability

by elongating the miracle fringe.

a beautiful city,

vast interior left   .

An age

of increment and evidence

the vox.

Expansive eras

deliver   that endure

erasure. Rote

mighty Liquid Paper, & ribbon

make the   a keeper.

I, CONIC

Begin with the 9th battalion, circa 1968—

    the trigger quiet as a cluster, designed to disfigure—

        Begin with the man designing the bomb in careful

    hand—his degree

    of innocence and oblivion—a room of women, men

gazing at images of the victims—the person

        who rebuilt her house after bombing seven—Begin

    with the 9th—tricking the gods within—with the

women,

    men asking the same question—with the redress

of sadness—with aberration if only in proportion—with

    the unbridled

        impulse of certain men—the distress of

    their mates, their friends—the witness from ten directions—

Begin

        with surviving to the end—the beautiful, ancient

    visages—

69

with "a state of very poor quality"—with revulsion—our
distance—

     "accelerated pacification"—
atrocity and its normalizations—the marriage of impunity and
retribution—

the speaker's trust—
     the evidence—
     the working condition—

THE GLASS AGE

Every age an age of glass: A slipper shoes
the foot, takes giant steps of tock and tick,
a cone blown, known gone, glass is fashioned, metal
spun to color, mineral made light,

and this is the last poem I will write.
Glass is sand is time falling loose,
a gap of glass is wrapping, a bottle
(   ) or swan (   ) of the human whose

hand will flip the glass, grabbing it
by the neck. Every time a nick.
And it is our glass to raise and smash.
A female silhouette, a shape, a vase

with two closed ends, one met. Two cones have kissed.
And the skin of our limit is glass.

FIX THE SPHINX

Addicted to riddle and reversals

of person. Shift happens.

Core pulled down to core.

      The monstrous breadth,

beached. The navel gazes

with its inner

whorl, eye knit over

original tore. The great draw

      at world's, at world's ignition.

A stutter burns the heavens,

as seizure grabs

the firmament's flotsam.

A tug at the wall of the mind's drum,

as the riddle resolves.

NOTES

Much gratitude to Guido Mocafico and Hamiltons Gallery for granting permission to feature his photograph of Leopold and Rudolf Blaschka's glass model of *Glaucus longicirrus* on the cover of this book. *Glaucus longicirrus* is a type of nudibranch or carnivorous, hermaphroditic sea slug. The Blaschkas were a late-19th-century father and son team of artisans who made an astonishing series of works in glass, mostly plants and invertebrate creatures, on commission for numerous institutions for scientific study. The Harvard Museum of Natural History's collection of the Blaschkas's "Glass Flowers" informs the poems in this collection, as do the glass works of other visual artists including Marcel Duchamp's *The Bride Stripped Bare by Her Bachelors, Even (The Large Glass)* and the sculptures of Louise Bourgeois.

The first epigraph is from Louis MacNeice's poem "Bagpipe Music" from *The Collected Poems of Louis MacNeice*, edited by E.R. Dodds (Faber & Faber, 2016). The quotation that opens section II is from Angela Carter's short story "The Bloody Chamber" found in the collection *The Bloody Chamber and Other Stories* (Penguin Books, 1990). The epigraph preceding section III comprises my own translation of the Korean proverb. Many thanks to Arlene Kim and Youna Kwak for their indispensable help with translating this saying.

For the evocations of the Greek myths, I drew upon many sources including the *Apollodorus: The Library of Greek Mythology*, translated and with an Introduction and Notes by Robin Hard (Oxford University Press, 2008) and *Euripides I: Four Tragedies: The Medea* translated by Rex Warner (University of Chicago Press, 1955).

In retelling the fairy tales, I reread an old, beloved copy of *Grimm's Fairy Tales Illustrated* (Airmont Publishing Company, 1968), *Jacob and Wilhelm Grimm: Selected Tales*, translated by Joyce Crick (Oxford University Press, 2009), and many other collections.

"The Iron Age" takes its cue from Nick Turse's writings on the Pentagon's efforts to weaponize cyborg insects. "I, Conic" responds to Nick's writings on war crimes committed by American soldiers during the Vietnam War, which are chronicled in his book *Kill Anything That Moves: The Real American War in Vietnam* (Metropolitan Books, 2013).

"Neptune Frost" was inspired by both the Greco-Roman god of the sea and the name and brief history of an African American slave and drummer who fought for the Continental Army during the Revolutionary War and who is buried with other soldiers in the Old Burying Ground in Cambridge, Massachusetts.

"The Ivory Box" is a collaboration with the sculptures of Mario d'Souza.

"Age of Increment" takes its cue and the word liberticide from Percy Bysshe Shelley's great sonnet "England in 1819," which begins with the line: "An old, mad, blind, despis'd, and dying king, . . ."

The sisters Goneril and Regan from William Shakespeare's *King Lear* narrate "I, Sororicide."

"The White Box" is inspired by the paintings of Ema Harris-Sintamarian.

"The Black Box" responds to the films of Felipe Pereira Barros.

"Zone Planning" loosely reimagines the figure of Satan from John Milton's *Paradise Lost*.

ACKNOWLEDGMENTS

This book was 14 years in the making from hem to haw and would not be what it is without the crucial advice, encouragement, and material and ethereal support of many individuals and institutions. First, I would like to thank the editors of the following journals who championed these poems early on and who first published them sometimes under different titles and in slightly different form:

Beloit Poetry Journal: "Age of Increment;" *Boston Review*: "A Parable;" *Conduit*: "For Sure;" *Cranky Literary Journal*: "The Red Box;" *Devil's Lake*: "The Copper Age;" *Drunken Boat*: "Reveille;" *Dusie*: "I, Conic;" *Ecotone*: "Yonder, A Rental;" *Exquisite Corpse*: "The Empress;" *Fairy Tale Review*: "Cin City;" *Fence*: "Zone Planning" and "Va-Va Psalm;" *Gargoyle Magazine*: "Snowem;" *The Gihon River Review*: "Winter Entry;" *Great River Review*: "Champion Under Wood;" *Green Mountains Review*: "F, H & G," "Spun," "Muse & Me," "The Peach Box," "Salomé," "The Iron Age," "The Platinum Age," "The Nights," "The Hood," "The Hologynic," "I, Tonic," "Box," and "Plainest Hymn;" *Harvard Review*: "Neptune Frost;" *jubilat*: "Latin Mass;" *Mandorla*: "The White Box," "Psyche," "The Green Box," "Moon to Sun," and "Echo;" *The Nation*: "I, Sing;" *New Orleans Review*: "The Bronze Age;" *No Tell Motel*: "Medea V/ Departure;" *Poetry*: "A Fable;" *POOL*: "Io," "Europa," "Demograph," "Persephone," "Cassandra," "Circe," "Pandora," "Minos," and "The Glass Age;" *The Quarry*: "I, Sing;" *Quarterly West*: "Fix the Sphinx" and "10 to 2;" *Revolting Sofas*: "The Red Box;" *Sonora Review*: "Clue;" *Southwest Review*: "Age of Evidence;" *Tarpaulin Sky*: "The Empress;" *Unsplendid*: "Chorus;" "Aura," "The Three Spinning-Women," and "Ever Your Mate;" *Wave Composition*: "I, Noumenal" and "I, Lyric."

Other poems were re-published in the following anthologies and venues:

The Best American Poetry: "A Parable" and "Yonder, A Rental;" *Best New Poets*: "Aura;" *Fire On Her Tongue: An Anthology of Contemporary Women's Poetry* (Two Sylvias Press, 2012): "Medea V/Departure;" *Verse Daily*: "Spun," "Age of Increment" and "Aura."

"I, Sing" appeared as a Poem-of-the-Week on the Split This Rock Poetry Festival site.

I am indebted to the Radcliffe Institute for Advanced Study for providing me with abundant space and time to draft, revise, and otherwise make and shape these poems. Conversations that I had with my fellow Radcliffe fellows directly informed the writing of this collection. "Plainest Hymn" is dedicated to Diana Sorensen, Taylor Davis, Amy Sillman, Susan Muller, Karen Kramer, Mignon Nixon, Irene Lusztig, Lynne Jones, Gene Jarrett, Don Berman, Kristen Ghodsee, and Barbara Weinstein.

A million thank you's also to Fundación Valparaíso, Kunstnarhuset Messen, Djerassi Resident Artists Program, the A Room of Her Own Foundation, and the Corporation of Yaddo for granting me residencies where I composed, revised, and read drafts of these poems to ideal audiences of writers and artists. Friendships that I made at these residencies also inform some of the collaborative poems in this collection. I am grateful to Ursinus College for supporting the revision and submission of this work and to my colleagues at Ursinus for their many kindnesses and good cheer.

My deepest gratitude to Joanna Klink, Liz Powell, and David Micah Greenberg for providing guidance with this collection at critical points in its evolution from manuscript to book. And special thanks to the Michener Center for Writers, Elizabeth Cullingford, and Tom Cable at the University of Texas for igniting my interest in the sonnet as a vehicle for personal and political expression.

Finally, a world of appreciation to Suzanne Buffam for selecting this collection for the Cleveland State University Poetry Center's First Book prize, to Caryl Pagel for her incredibly generous and astute insights into the manuscript, to Amy Freels for the beautiful cover and book design, and to everyone at the CSU Poetry Center. It has been a true pleasure to work with you from start to finish and an honor to be among the CSU Poetry Center's poets and writers.

"A Parable" is for David Lehman.
"The Platinum Age" is for Daphne Brooks.
"The Iron Age" is for Nick Turse.
"The Bronze Age" is for Rick Kenney.
"Neptune Frost" is for David Micah Greenberg.
"The Ivory Box" is for Mario d'Souza.
"Io" is for Karen Russell.
"Circe" is for Judith Taylor.
"Pandora" is for Kathryn Goettl.
"Chorus" is for Christopher Wendell Jones and Ann Yi.
"Medea V/Departure" is for Maureen McLane.
"Spun" is for Rachel Levitsky.
"Cin City" is dedicated to the memory of Chana Bloch.
"F, H & G" is for Marla Akin.
"The Three Spinning-Women" is for Ida Stewart.
"I, Sororicide" is for Emily Weissbourd.
"Reveille" is for Michelle Chan Brown.
"Aura" is for Douglas Basford and Jason Gray.

"The White Box" is for Ema Harris-Sintamarian.

"Salomé" is for Katarina Burin and Matt Saunders.

"The Nights" is for Jeanne Heuving.

"The Empress" is for Alan Lau and Kazuko Nakane.

"Champion Under Wood" is for Dean Taylor.

"Winter Entry" is for Philip Pardi.

"Psyche" is for Rosa Alcalá.

"The Black Box" is for James Hannaham.

"I, Lyric" is for Joanna Klink.

"Minos" is for Charles Mudede.

"Yonder, A Rental" is for Shawn Wong and Erin Malone.

"10 to 2" is for Jessica Rae Bergamino.

"Demograph" is for Perry Sayles and Steve Harvey.

"Latin Mass" is for Heather McHugh.

"The Glass Age" is for Liz Powell.